JOHN
MUIR

JOHN MUIR

Wilderness Prophet

by
Peter Anderson

A First Book
Franklin Watts
A Division of Grolier Publishing
New York / London / Hong Kong / Sydney
Danbury, Connecticut

Cover photographs copyright ©: B.A. DeWitt/Comstock, Inc.;
The Bettmann Archive (portrait)

Photographs copyright ©: Colby Memorial Library, Sierra Club: pp. 2, 34, 55;
John Muir Papers, Holt-Atherton Department of Special Collections, University of the
Pacifics Library, 1984, Muir-Hanna Trust: pp. 8, 10, 14, 15, 16, 26, 40, 44, 46, 47;
North Wind Picture Archives: pp. 12, 30; State Historical Society of Wisconsin:
p. 22 (WHi-X3-49855); University of Wisconsin-Madison Archives: p. 24 (X25-2315);
Jeff Foott Productions: p. 35; The Bettmann Archive: pp. 37, 56, 58; Ben Klaffke: pp. 48, 52.

Library of Congress Cataloging-in-Publication Data

Anderson, Peter, 1956–
John Muir : wilderness prophet / by Peter Anderson.
p. cm. — (A First book)
Includes bibliographical references (p.) and index.
ISBN 0-531-20204-6
1. Muir, John, 1838–1914—Juvenile literature
2. Naturalists—United States—Biography—Juvenile literature.
3. Conservationists—United States—Biography—Juvenile literature.
[1. Muir, John, 1838–1914. 2. Naturalists.
3. Conservationists.] I. Title. II. Series.
QH31.M9A54 1995
333.7'2'092—dc20

[B]   95-2598 CIP
                                                                           AC

CONTENTS

CHAPTER ONE

WANDERLUST

I loved to wander in the fields to hear the birds sing, and . . . to gaze and wonder at the . . . eels and crabs in the pools . . . when the tide was low; and best of all to watch the waves in awful storms thundering on the black headlands and craggy ruins of the old Dunbar Castle.

—John Muir

For John Muir, there was a time when the garden was enough. It was enough that his father had given him a handful of seeds and his own plot of land. It was enough to examine those hard, dry seeds and watch them as

John Muir spent his early years in Scotland. He later moved to the United States with his family.

they grew into plants with soft leaves and bright flowers.

Each day, as his beans and peas slowly took root, he dug them up to see how they had changed. And each day, after careful examination, he replanted them. For John Muir, this tiny patch of garden held a universe of wonders. So, it seemed, would the rugged Scottish headlands beyond the garden walls.

To venture beyond the garden walls, however, was to risk his father's wrath. Daniel Muir did not allow his children much idle time, nor did he allow them to roam the countryside as they pleased. If John was caught playing beyond the boundary of his own backyard, he could expect to feel the sting of his father's leather strap.

Despite the threat of such punishment, John could not deny his yearnings. On days when Daniel Muir was either traveling or too busy to notice, John and his brother, David, slipped away into the fields. Sometimes they met up with their free-roaming friends and ventured up to the craggy remains of the old Dunbar Castle.

Perched on a black-rock bluff above the North Sea, Dunbar Castle had weathered over a thousand years of fierce storms that battered the coastline. Legends of great battles fought to defend the castle from foreign marauders only added to the joys of

Young John Muir was rarely allowed to stray
far from his family's home in Scotland.

climbing up the ancient remains of its stairways and towers.

One day, John and his friends found the entrance to a sea cave along a narrow strip of beach below the castle. In flickering candlelight, John led his friends through the dank salty air of the cave. Years and years of pounding surf, they soon found out, had carved the cave all the way into the castle's dungeons. As their shadows wobbled on the black rock walls, John led his friends past the bones of long-dead prisoners.

Even at the age of nine, danger seemed to tempt John Muir. When he found a gaping black hole in the dungeon floor, he crept down over the edge and into the darkness, daring his friends to follow. As he dug his toes and fingers into the cracks of the stone walls, he sank farther into the depths of what seemed like a bottomless pit. Light from the candles above him grew faint. His hands and legs shook with fatigue. How much longer could he hold on?

Finally, in almost total darkness, he stepped onto solid ground. Later on, when he emerged from the pit, he was breathless and covered with cobwebs. His great smile sparkled in the glow of the candles. No one had matched his dare.

Back home later that day, John was told that he would end up in Hell if he didn't behave

He did, however, find danger and adventure
in a cave near the ancient Dunbar Castle.

himself. "Maybe so," he said, "but if I do I'll climb
right out again."

CHAPTER TWO

GOD'S PROPERTY

I was put to the plough at the age of twelve, when my head reached little above the handles.
—John Muir

In the winter of 1849, Daniel Muir's decision to move his family to America came as joyful news to his eleven-year-old son. Out on the frontier, there would be endless wild lands to explore, not to mention all the birds and animals that John had studied in the books of John James Audubon, the famous American artist. Best of all, there wouldn't be any school lessons to worry about.

John's parents, Daniel

and Ann Muir.

The Bur-oak Shanty. Wisconsin
Our first American home

This sketch by John Muir
shows the family's first house in Wisconsin.

"Poor laddies, you'll find something else over the sea besides . . . bird's nests and freedom from lessons," warned John's grandfather as he listened to the Muir boys talking excitedly about leaving for America. "You'll find plenty of hard, hard work!"

And indeed they did. Because John was the oldest son, most of the farm work on the Muir homestead in Wisconsin fell on his shoulders. It was a heavy burden for a scrawny twelve-year-old. Often breathless and aching from long hours of wrestling with the ox-driven plow, John plodded through the fields day after day.

Farm work was hardest during the summer months, when the fields were draped with hot, humid air. Chores, which included chopping wood, feeding animals, and carrying water up from the spring, began at four o'clock in the morning. After breakfast, John cut wheat under the broiling sun. Often, it wasn't until dusk that he was able to break for supper. After evening chores, he struggled to stay awake as his father read to the family from the Bible.

Still, as hard as the work was, moments of grace and beauty were not lost on him. While Daniel Muir introduced John to discipline, hard work, and the Bible, his mother taught him to appreciate his surroundings. Hard work never kept John from tasting the strawberries that grew underneath the meadow grasses, or listening to the robins that filled the oak groves with their loud cheerful songs, or watching the fireflies that sprinkled light into the sultry summer evenings.

Such wonders offered John some relief from his father's demands. "You are God's property," Daniel Muir often told his children as they labored in his fields. If that was so, John wondered, then why wasn't he treated with more respect?

Once, when John was sick with the mumps and unable to swallow solid food, his father still made him work a full day in the fields. God and hard work, said his father, were by far the best doctors. And when it came time to dig a new well, Daniel insisted that his son carve it out with a hammer and a mason's chisel. Day after day, John rode a bucket into the darkness of the narrow shaft. There, in a space little more than 3 feet (.9 m) wide, he chiseled ever deeper into a bed of solid sandstone.

One morning, some 80 feet (24 m) into the earth, John began to feel dizzy. His knees buckled. The blurry circle of light at the top of the shaft seemed to swirl above him. Slumped over against the wall of the shaft, John called out for help in a voice so faint he doubted anyone would hear him.

Luckily, Daniel Muir was nearby. He could barely see his son doubled over at the bottom of the shaft. "Get in the bucket and hold on," he yelled. He began to pull the bucket up but John wasn't in it.

Again he called to his son. By now John was so dizzy and disoriented he was barely able to find his way into the bucket. By the time his father had raised him up out of the well, John was sick and gasping for air.

"Weel Johnnie, it's God's mercy you're alive," said William Duncan, a neighborly Scotsman who came by shortly after the accident. As a former miner, Duncan knew plenty of men who had died breathing poisonous gases underground. It seemed especially cruel that a boy as young as John had almost died the same way. Duncan made sure that Daniel Muir cleared the bad air out of the shaft. It was lucky for John that he did.

Only a few days after the accident, John still felt weak and wobbly, but his father insisted that he finish digging the well. So he rode into the darkness once again and chipped away at the hard sandstone. Several days later, and some 10 feet (3 m) deeper, he finally struck water. One last time he rode the bucket into daylight, grateful to have finished a job that had almost killed him.

A RESTLESS MIND

When I was about fifteen or sixteen years of age, I began to grow hungry for real knowledge.
—John Muir

If there was a bright side to the dark experience of digging his father's well, it was making the acquaintance of William Duncan. Duncan had great sympathy and respect for the oldest of the Muir boys. He knew that John did the work of two men. He also knew that John loved to read. So he occasionally drove his oxen by the Muir place in the evenings to bring the boy new books.

Even though Daniel Muir expected his children to go straight to bed after family worship in the evenings, John often lingered in the kitchen with a book and a candle. If he could get five minutes of reading in before his father noticed, he considered himself lucky.

One winter night, Daniel Muir grew tired of John's evening routine. "Must I give you a separate order every night to go to bed?" he growled. Then he noticed that John was reading a church history. "Well, if you will read," he continued in a softer tone, "get up in the morning . . . you may get up as early as you like."

Those words changed John's life. To have free time to read—what a luxury! Never mind that it meant getting up at one o'clock in the morning and reading by the light of a candle in a freezing cold basement. Free time like this seemed too good to be true.

John began to worry that his father might object to the extra firewood that he burned to warm himself on those frosty mornings. So he went to work with some simple tools—a couple of files, a hammer, a chisel, and a saw that he made from a scrap of steel—and built a model for a sawmill. It was one of many inventions that John would come up with as he read and read and continued to tinker in his basement workshop over the next few years.

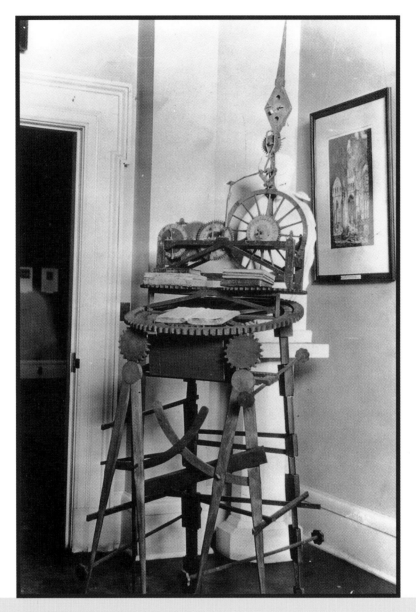

This clock and desk was one of the many clever inventions
John Muir conjured up during the early morning hours.

William Duncan was among those who began to take notice of John's creative and mechanical talents. He marveled at the clocks that John designed and whittled out of wood. He admired the thermometers and barometers, the waterwheels, the automatic lamp and fire lighters. John had even designed a tilting bed that automatically got him up in the morning. With Duncan's encouragement, John left home in 1860 to take his inventions to the Wisconsin State Fair in Madison.

As wheels and levers turned and creaked and his trick bed tipped up and dumped its sleeper onto the floor, crowds of admirers laughed and applauded John's display at the fair. Newspaper reporters marveled at this twenty-two-year-old farm lad who seemed to have such a knack for inventing.

In a letter to his sister, John wrote of his first experience away from home: "For three of four days my eyes were pleased and teased and wearied" by swarms of fair-goers and the exhibits they had come to see. But more than anything, it was the University of Wisconsin in Madison that caught John's attention.

Over the next few years John would feed his hunger for knowledge in the classrooms and libraries of the university. Botany studies, along with other courses in physics, geology, and chemistry, inspired him to take long wandering field trips

John attended the University of Wisconsin
at Madison.

through the forests of the Midwest. Whenever his money ran out, he took temporary jobs at farms, mills, and factories.

In the spring of 1867, John was working late at a carriage factory in Indianapolis when his world, all of a sudden, went dark. He was trying to adjust a pulley belt with a file when his hand slipped. The file handle pierced his right eye. The shock of the accident blinded his left eye. For several weeks, he lay on his back in a dark room wondering if his eyesight would return.

About a month after the accident, John's vision gradually returned. On his first walk through the woods, he savored the trees and sky as if seeing them for the first time. The owners of the factory had promised him shorter work days and a large raise in salary. They had also assured him of a partnership in their business someday, but John could not be tempted. He would devote himself to the "University of the Wilderness." There, in America's mountains and forests, he would study the creations of God.

John Muir as a young man.

CHAPTER FOUR

UNIVERSITY OF THE WILDERNESS

I could have been a millionaire . . . I chose to become a tramp.
— John Muir

Shortly after his vision returned, John made plans for a trek to the Gulf of Mexico, perhaps continuing as far south as the jungles of the Amazon. The University of the Wilderness was to be his classroom and his workplace, but first he would bid his family farewell.

His father's criticisms overshadowed the joy and warmth he felt back home with the rest of his family and friends. Daniel Muir continually nagged John during his visit, complaining that his studies would lead him "down the devil's path." To study nature, John argued, was to honor God's creation. How could he be any closer to God than that?

Daniel Muir's criticisms never let up. On the day of his departure, John was saying good-bye to his mother and sisters when his father interrupted. "My son, have you not forgotten something?"

"What have I forgotten, Father?"

"Have you not forgotten to pay for your board and lodging?"

"You asked me to come home for a visit. I thought I was welcome, " John said, handing his father a gold coin. "You may be very sure it will be a long time before I come again."

On September 3, 1867, twenty-nine-year-old John Muir set off on his southward trek. It was just the beginning of a long journey that would lead him to lands far beyond the horizons that had rimmed his Wisconsin boyhood. His plan, he wrote, as he walked south to Indiana and then into the rolling hills of Kentucky, was to travel "the wildest, leafiest, least trodden way" he could find.

Along the way, he would often seek out shelter and hospitality from those few families who lived along his wilderness route. One night in

Kentucky, he stayed with a blacksmith who wondered why he was traveling alone in such wild country. John replied that he was looking for plants.

"Surely you are able to do something better than wander over the country to look at weeds and blossoms," quipped the blacksmith.

John responded by reminding his host of the value that Jesus Christ had seen in such work: "Remember that Christ told his disciples to 'consider the lilies as they grow.' You say don't consider them. It isn't worthwhile . . . whose advice am I to take?" That seemed to satisfy his host who later wished him the best and warned him of robbers who roamed the area.

Several days later, John saw ten men approaching him on horseback. If these men were the robbers that he had heard about, there wasn't much he could do other than to face them with all the confidence he could muster. "Howdy," he bellowed, as he walked up and around them without breaking stride. The ten men only watched as this ragged man hiked by, figuring perhaps that he was too poor to rob.

Robbers were only one of John's concerns as he journeyed deeper into the South. Local people warned him of snakes, alligators, and even ghosts that inhabited the black water swamps he wandered through. There were times when the dense thorny vines and the dark muck of the swamplands tried his nerves. Still, the strange new plants and animals intrigued him.

When he reached Savannah, Georgia, on October 8, John was weary and almost out of

Nearly out of money, Muir camped on the outskirts of Savannah, Georgia, during his journey south.

money. He camped in a cemetery on the outskirts of town and lived on little more than water and a few stale crackers until the money his brother had promised to send finally arrived. He celebrated with a feast of gingerbread and left soon after on a boat bound for Florida.

By the time he arrived on the Gulf Coast of Florida later that fall, John had walked more than a 1,000 miles (1,600 km). One day in the Florida town of Cedar Keys, he was inquiring at a sawmill about passage on a boat carrying lumber to Cuba, when all those miles seemed to catch up with him. First he noticed a numbness in his limbs, then a headache that wouldn't go away. The fever that followed left him weak and delirious for several months.

As he recovered in the home of the gracious sawmill owner who took him in, John grew restless. One day, he noticed the sails of a large schooner approaching the harbor. Despite the protests of his hosts, who thought him too sick to travel, John thanked them, bid them farewell, walked down to the harbor, and boarded the ship that was bound for Cuba.

ANYWHERE WILD

As long as I live, I'll hear waterfalls and birds and wind sing. I'll interpret the rocks, learn the language of flood, storm and the avalanche. I'll acquaint myself with the glaciers and wild gardens, and get as near the heart of the world as I can.
—John Muir

If John Muir had been able to, he would have climbed inside a blooming flower. He would have hitched a ride on a snowflake or ridden a drop of water down a cascade. The closer he could get to the heart of world, he believed, the closer he would get to God.

In January 1868, as wind whipped up the Caribbean and sheets of rain slashed the deck, the captain of the Island Belle urged John to wait out the storm in the cabin below. Despite his lingering fever, John refused to leave the deck. He grabbed a rope and held on through the storm, breathing in the ocean fury he had once known as a young boy sailing to America.

As able as he was to withstand the cold and the wind on his journey to Cuba, he couldn't seem to shake the fever that had dogged him for several months. After five or six relapses in Havana, he decided to leave the tropics. Perhaps it would take the colder air of northern mountains—mountains such as the Sierra Nevada of California—to rid him of these tropical germs.

After a series of long and crowded boat rides, north to New York, south to the isthmus of Panama, then up the west coast of South America and Mexico, John arrived in San Francisco. He asked a man on the wharf for the quickest route out of the city.

"Where do you want to go?" the man asked him.

"Anywhere that is wild," John replied. Several weeks later, he stood on Pacheco Pass, looking down on the flowered fields of California's Central Valley and beyond to the peaks of the Sierra Nevada. Here was the wild side of the continent that he had been seeking.

John Muir arrived in the Sierra Nevada region of
California in 1868 and was swept away by the beauty of
the mountainous landscape.

That summer, he took a job herding sheep
across the high meadows of the Sierras where

Muir's love of the natural world led to an all-too-close encounter with a California brown bear.

mountain air and icy streams seemed once and for all to cool his fever. At first, the grandeur of the landscape overwhelmed him—the mountains were so much bigger than any he had ever seen. Nevertheless, as had often been the case during his travels, John was determined to know the "heart" of this place.

One day, while walking through a stand of fir trees, he spotted a California brown bear out in the middle of a nearby meadow. He decided to get a closer look.

The bear stood on its hind legs sniffing the air. It must have weighed at least 500 pounds (185 kg), he figured. Anxious to see it run, John dashed out of the pines shouting and waving his arms. He had heard that California brown bears usually ran away from humans, but this bear wasn't that shy. It just lowered its shaggy head and stared right at him.

By now, John was too close to try to outrun the beast. All he could do was freeze in his tracks and stare right back.

For what seemed like hours he stared back, trying to match the bear's fierce gaze with one of his own. Slowly, the bear turned away. Slowly, it walked away through a swath of wildflowers. Slowly, it disappeared over a hill.

"In the great canon's," John later wrote, "Bruin reigns supreme.

Like these brave Yosemite hikers, John Muir explored
and studied every nook and cranny of the region.

VISIONS OF STONE AND ICE

CHAPTER SIX

The mountains are calling me and I must go.
—John Muir

Perched on the high peaks above the Yosemite Valley, looking out over domes and pinnacles of granite, over canyons, and cliffs and waterfalls, John Muir knew that the story of this landscape was written in stone. To know this place, he would have to learn the language of the rocks. To learn that language, he began asking questions that only the land could answer.

He wondered about the grooves he found gouged out of the granite floor of a canyon above the valley. What forces, he wondered, could have carved this rock? And what about the huge boulders he found—the ones that looked so out of place—perched by themselves on rock made up of such different minerals? Had they come from somewhere else? If so, what could have carried them?

Gradually, what he saw in Yosemite and what he remembered from the geology of Wisconsin combined to give him some answers. Rocks cemented in the moving ice of a glacier, he figured, could have carved out the grooves in the canyon floor. A glacier must have carried the bigger boulders down from the mountains, leaving them behind when it melted. And if there had been ice and snow enough to carry these boulders, maybe the same glaciers had carved out the Yosemite Valley.

Whenever he could break away from his job at a local sawmill, John climbed the ridges and peaks surrounding Yosemite, seeking out further evidence of glaciers. As a guide leading tourists up and down the valley trails in the spring of 1869, he shared his ideas with anyone who seemed interested. At night his dreams were filled with visions of stone and ice.

Not all of those who heard of John's theories agreed with them, least of all Josiah Whitney, the California state geologist. "What does that sheepherder know?" Whitney snapped. As far as he was concerned, the deep valley of Yosemite wasn't

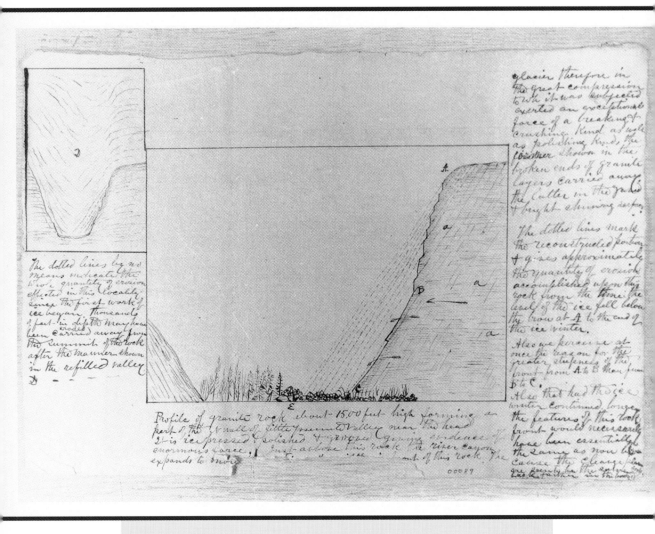

John Muir made many sketches of the
Yosemite landscape and wrote long notes
detailing his observations.

scooped out by rivers of ice, rock, and snow. Nor had there ever been any glaciers in the High Sierra. The landscape of Yosemite, he claimed, was shaped by a shifting in the earth's crust that had caused the valley floor to sink.

Josiah Whitney may have been a Harvard professor and a professional geologist, but John believed that he was wrong about Yosemite. On July 10, 1869, John sawed his last log at the mill and settled up with his boss. With little more than a blanket and several loaves of bread, he disappeared into the mountains. He was determined to resolve the question of High Sierra glaciers once and for all.

For the next few months, John hiked canyon after canyon, tracing back what he believed to be the "writing" of ancient ice flows. On the few occasions when he came down from the mountains to replenish his food supply, John's clothes were tattered. His clear blue eyes were nearly hidden by a wild tangle of hair and beard. His face was darkened with soot to protect him from the mountain sun. Few of those who saw him would have guessed that he was about to make an important scientific discovery.

On the morning of October 6, John was following a stream up a dark canyon high in the Sierra, when he noticed the water turning gray. He dipped his hands in the stream. A fine gray silt covered his fingers. It was gritty like ground-up stone. Up ahead, he could see that the stream gurgled out from underneath a huge wall of boulders some 60 feet (18 m) high.

He climbed up the boulder pile. At the top was a layer of ice crystals, something like hail, that continued up the canyon and disappeared in the shadows of a large black mountain. Ahead of him was a deep crevice. He crawled along the edge, peering down into deeper layers of rock and ice. Never had he seen anything like this before.

John zigged and zagged down the frozen walls of the crack until he had reached the deep blue ice at the bottom. From there, he could see only a narrow sliver of sky. He listened to the water dripping down from the icicles above him. He listened to the murmur of the hidden stream below. He listened to himself breathe in the heart of a living glacier.

CHAPTER SEVEN

FOREVER A MOUN- TAINEER

*I am hopelessly and forever
a mountaineer.*
—John Muir

In that icy blue cavern high above Yosemite, John Muir found the answer to riddles carved in stone. His discovery of the first glacier in the High Sierra would earn him a reputation with scientists nationwide. And it would deepen his bond with the mountains and valleys that were beginning to feel like his home.

The Sierra Nevada, mountains that had once seemed so vast, even threatening, had become his refuge, even his temple. The high ridges and peaks

seemed to glow as if glazed by the sun. To bask in that light was one of John's great joys. The steeper the climb, the better.

As a companion once put it, John scaled the cliffs of the High Sierra "like a human spider." But as he approached the summit of Mt. Ritter in October 1872, it appeared as though he had "spun a web" that he was unable to escape. Halfway up an icy cliff face, he was clinging to the rock, unable to move his feet or hands in any direction. He broke into a cold sweat. His legs quivered. He imagined himself falling to the glacier below.

Then his thoughts went blank except for the rock wall in front of him. Now he saw the rock as if he was looking through a magnifying glass. Where before it had seemed flat and smooth, now there were tiny cracks, just big enough to wedge a fingertip into. Feeling a great surge of strength and confidence, he scrambled up to a summit that no one had yet climbed and basked in the glow of the mountain.

It was this kind of experience that would call John back, again and again, to the roof of the High Sierra. But there were other yearnings, like the longing for friends and family, that called to him as well. Visits to San Francisco during the winter months when Yosemite's population dwindled, became more frequent. It was through friends in the city that he

John Muir married Louise Strentzel in 1880.

The couple had two daughters, Wanda and Helen.

John Muir lived with his family in this house
in Martinez, California.

would meet Louise Strentzel, the woman he married in the spring of 1880.

For a while, it appeared as though John would be happy enough managing the orchards on the Strentzel family ranch. The longing for a partner seemed stronger than his urge for the wilderness. Then, in August 1885, another urge took John by surprise. He had been reading in his study when he was struck by the notion that his father was dying. He had heard nothing of the sort from other family members, but these troubling thoughts were too strong to ignore.

On September 24, John arrived at Daniel Muir's bedside. He had been sick, John's sister said, for about a month. John sat by his father's bed, holding the old man's hand. "Is this my dear John?" his father asked from his fevery haze.

"Just as you're a Scotchman," John said.

"My dear wanderer," Daniel muttered. With a low moaning sound, he drew his son closer and held him tight.

Right around midnight several nights later, John saw his father's eyes close for the last time. As the grieving family gathered in the dimly lit bedroom, it was John who spoke out. "In all our devious ways and wanderings," he said, "we have loved one another."

Balancing a devotion to family with a yearning to wander had never been easy for John. Back in California, it became increasingly difficult. The harder he worked on the Strentzel family ranch, the worse his health became. He coughed constantly. He grew skinny and frail. Finally, Louise insisted that he return to the mountains to restore his health.

Wilderness was as good a remedy as any for John Muir. Again and again, mountain treks seemed to heal him of the allergies that plagued him in the lowlands. With Louise's support, John wrote his own prescription whenever his health began to fail him. Once, when he planned a journey to Alaska to regain his sagging strength, his doctor advised against it.

"If you go on that journey," the doctor said, "you'll pay for it with your life."

"If I don't go," said John, "I'll pay for it with my life."

CHAPTER EIGHT

WILDLANDS CRUSADER

In God's wildness lies the hope of the world.
—John Muir

To all who would listen, John Muir preached the gospel of the wilderness. Time in the mountains renewed his body and his spirit. In his writings, he wished the same for others: "Climb the mountains and get their good tidings," he told his readers. "Nature's peace will flow into you as sunshine flows into trees. "

Unlike most of his mountain visits, John found little to be joyful about when he trekked through Yosemite in June 1889. Even though it had been set

At this desk, Muir wrote many influential
articles advocating the preservation of
natural wonders like Yosemite.

aside as a state park in 1866, Yosemite was under attack. Where once there had been tall trees, now there were only charred stumps. Meadows once lush and green had been grazed as bare as the streets of San Francisco. Something had to be done, but what?

Late one night around a campfire, John agreed to write several articles in defense of Yosemite. It wouldn't be the first time he had written on behalf of the land. Over the years, John's writings had earned him fame as a naturalist and an advocate for preserving wildlands.

John had spoken out in defense of Yosemite before too, but now it seemed especially urgent. Shortly after his articles were published, they were reprinted in newspapers and magazines nationwide. Letters began to pour into Washington supporting the establishment of Yosemite National Park. On October 1, 1890, the bill was passed and signed by President Benjamin Harrison, but the battle for Yosemite wasn't over.

Opponents of the park argued that resources for timber and grazing in Yosemite were more valuable than wildlands and scenery ever could be. They continued to pressure Congress, demanding that the park be cut in half. In 1892, Congress passed a bill that would do just that. But before it could reach the Senate, John Muir mounted a campaign of his own.

In May 1892, recognizing the need for an organization that would fight to preserve some of California's wildlands, John and several of his close friends founded the Sierra Club. In the battle against Congress, John rallied members of the newly formed club to speak out for Yosemite. Taking advantage of his national reputation, he gave interviews to newspapers across the country. Members of the Senate, feeling pressured by the letters that poured into their offices, voted down the bill the House of Representatives had passed. Yosemite National Park survived intact.

It had been a sweet victory for John, but it was only a temporary one. As John Muir neared the end of his life, he would face his toughest loss in the battle over Yosemite. James D. Phelan, the mayor of San Francisco, had proposed to build a city reservoir inside the park boundary. John maintained that this kind of project would not only desecrate Yosemite, it would open the door to the violation of other

John Muir and a gathering of Sierra Club members at Yosemite in approximately 1906. Today, Muir's Sierra Club is one of the most powerful environmental organizations in the United States.

John Muir became a successful activist in the fight to
preserve the nation's wild lands. Here, he poses with
President Theodore Roosevelt in 1903.

national parks. Besides, he argued, there were other ways for San Francisco to create a dependable water supply.

John wrote and spoke tirelessly in defense of Hetch Hetchy, the valley to be flooded if Mayor Phelan got his way. When presidents Theodore Roosevelt and William Taft came out to tour Yosemite, John guided and befriended them and argued the case for preservation with passion.

In the end, efforts to save Hetch Hetchy weren't enough. The dam was built, the valley flooded. It had been a demanding fight and bitter disappointment, but John's spirit wasn't broken. He would continue to speak out and stand up for the wildlands that he had dedicated his life to. He would continue to blaze a trail for other Americans who would go on to defend the value of national parks and wildlands.

It had been said of John that a whole continent couldn't satisfy his lust for exploring wildlands. In the last few years preceding his death in 1914, he would prove that to be true, wandering as far afield as Africa and South America.

In Brazil, responding to a newspaper reporter's question, John said that he had no plans to do any more writing until he gave up his current occupation.

"And what might that be?" asked the reporter.

"Tramp," said John. "I'm seventy-four and still good at it."

FOR FURTHER READING

Amdur, Richard. *Wilderness Preservation*. New York: Chelsea House Publishers, 1993.

Challand, Helen J. *Vanishing Forests*. Chicago: Childrens Press, 1991.

Douglas, William O. *Muir of the Mountains*. San Francisco: Sierra Club Books for Children, 1994.

Faber, Doris. *Nature and the Environment*. New York: Scribner, 1991.

Hirsch, S. Carl. *Guardians of Tomorrow: Pioneers in Ecology*. New York: Viking Press, 1971.

Keene, Ann T. *Earthkeepers: Observers and Protectors of Nature*. New York: Oxford University Press, 1994.

Talmadge, Katherine S. *John Muir: At Home in the Wild*. New York: Twenty-First Century Books, 1993.

Wadsworth, Ginger. *John Muir: Wilderness Protector*. Minneapolis: Lerner Publications Co., 1992.

INDEX

ABOUT THE AUTHOR

Peter Anderson has worked as a river guide, carpenter, newspaper reporter, writing teacher, editor, and wilderness ranger. He has written ten books for young readers on topics related to nature, Native Amer-icans, and the history of the American West. Currently, he lives in Salt Lake City, Utah.